Wine

A Pocket Guide Club Guide

Pocket Guide Club

ISBN: 1732013713
ISBN-978-1-7320137-1-1

THANK YOU

By purchasing this guide you've helped get an additional guide into the hands of someone else. The guides we giveaway are on important life skills, from personal finance and money management to self-discipline and leadership. Your purchase makes a difference in the life of someone else. Thank you.

CONTENTS

INTRODUCTION

Did you know wine is good for you?

A substantial body of research out there proves it. By drinking just one to two glasses of wine a day—not more—researchers have found you can reduce your risk of developing type two diabetes and your risk of having a heart attack by more than 30 percent.

But wait. It doesn't stop there.

Drinking a glass or two of wine a day can cut your chances of having a blood-clot related stroke nearly in half, one study showed; make it red wine and you will reduce your chance of developing colon cancer by the same rate.

Studies and reports offer a lot of convincing health benefits, but there are plenty of obvious reasons to drink wine. It tastes good, can make your favorite food taste even better, and—it's been proven—to improve your mood, too.

But, before we get to all the different types of wines, let's take a look back to see where our relationship with wine all began.

Wine has been an integral part of our world

history since our earliest roots, and once you discover the origin of wine, I'm certain you'll enjoy that next glass so much more.

At the very least, friends and family thinking will think you're a sommelier!

2 HISTORY OF WINE

Much like the theories that point to the early beginnings of cheese as accidental, which you can see in our guide *On Cheese*, there's no doubt wine was a mistake as well, discovered after the accidental ingestion of fermented grapes.

Evidence of wine making has been found in areas in present day Armenia, Turkey, China, and Iran ten thousand years old.

In ancient Greece, around 500 BCE, partaking of wine was a major feature in men's Symposions, or drinking parties. The men, usually numbering at least nine or ten, would lie on benches around the walls of the room, which in the homes of the well-heeled was a space designated for just such activities called the andron, sort of an early forerunner of the man-cave.

There were strict rules regarding the amount of wine served to ensure all who gathered reached an equal and perfect degree of intoxication—but, as might be expected, things did not always go as planned. Activities centered around serious conversations; in fact, some of Plato's dialogues were first conceived at Symposions.

But there was another less intellectual activity, but certainly as popular, a drinking game called Kottabos. It went like this: when you had drained your shallow drinking cup, called a kylix, down to the dregs and sediment in the bottom, you would spin it and then flick the remains towards a target.

Sometime the target was a small metal disk that would fall and make a clunking sound if you were successful. Other times they aimed for small clay vessels to sink in a pool of water. Just to add to the level of difficulty, as you were hurling your dregs, you had to call out the name of your secret love. Hitting the target would be a good omen for your future love life, and it could win you a prize to boot.

Women were not allowed in these Symposions, except as entertainment, nor were they permitted to drink wine in ancient Rome either. One reason they were denied imbibing was that the Roman (male) ruling classes reportedly believed they were protecting women from slipping into debauchery. But not all women at the time got that message. One in particular, with close ties to Rome, was particularly fond of her wine.

Cleopatra VII, the last queen of Egypt, was a shrewd politician of Greek and Macedonian descent; she spoke seven languages, including Egyptian, a rarity for a Ptolemy. Though there were no grapes native to Egypt, vines had been transplanted and carefully tended on methodically placed arbors by royal winemakers in the Delta regions. Wine was a drink for the wealthy (beer for the masses), and banquets, where the wine flowed more freely than water, were the rage. Some even believed drinking wine led to greater communion with the gods.

Cleopatra, and her third husband, Roman Mark Antony, formed a secret drinking society called "inimitable livers" which some claim was a group devoted to Dionysus (the goddess of wine) and some say was just an excuse to party. After making a bet with Antony that she could spend 10 million sesterces (around $500,000) one just meal, she proved her worth during the second course.

According to Pliny the Elder, writing just a few decades after her death, Cleopatra was wearing two pearl earrings, reported to be the largest pearls in the world, when she lazily reached up, removed one, and plunked it into a cup of wine vinegar.

Theoretically, it dissolved and she drank it. She proved her point and won the bet.

"Cleopatra's Banquet" by Gerard de Lairesse (1675), from the Rijksmuseum

Fast forward ahead a bit to the French countryside in 1688 and the Benedictine abbey of Saint Pierre d'Hautvillers. A robed monk sips a glass of sparkling wine and utters the infamous words, "Come quickly! I am drinking the stars!"

You know the monk, Dom Pierre Pérignon, you know the region, Champagne, but you may not know that the words are, sadly, purely apocryphal, invented in the early nineteenth century by a manager at the same monastery no doubt trying to beef up business.

But, as with most good legends, there are pockets of truth contained within. Yes, there was indeed a Dom Pérignon, who lived in Champagne and who did in fact 'write the book' on bubbly. But that was not his original intent.

The Champagne region, in northeast France, has a colder climate and shorter growing season than other grape-growing regions in France.

As a result, grapes are often picked late. This means the yeast in the grapes do not have time to fully convert their sugars. So when spring comes, fermentation starts again—in the bottle. This creates carbon dioxide, aka bubbles. This could be a fearful thing. In fact monks who tended the wine cellars were always wary of this 'mad wine' that could easily explode and some took to wearing metal face masks to prevent damage from any occasional explosion of a vin du diable (devil's wine).

As to who first tamed the bubbles, it looks like credit may have to be given to—sacre bleu!—the English. Almost a hundred years prior they had invented a bottle with thick enough glass and a tied down cork that could contain the effervescence. But to get back to Dom P, though he may not have invented the bottling of sparkling wine, he mastered it. He had extensive vinicultural knowledge, was an expert at blending wines, and perfected a bright white wine good enough for the table of the Sun King, Louis XIV.

He put to use those bottles invented by the English and used Spanish cork as a stopper (as opposed to the wood and hemp more usually used). Above all, it was Pérignon who mastered the art of getting white wine from black grapes (two of the three grapes used in Champagne are black—Pinot Noir and Pinot Meunier).

Wine is still made the way he wrote down over three hundred years ago, and to that we owe him a toast.

3 SCIENCE OF WINE

The details required for making bubblies, Pérignon's methode champenoise, are unsurprisingly quite specialized. But making most wine follows the simple patterns set about thousands of years ago: pick, stomp, ferment, age, bottle. Granted, there are, however, many many variations within those steps. A good thing too as it means we all can find a wine we truly love.

The first step—picking the grapes—may seem simple. Though some smaller vineyards still pick by hand, most larger vineyards now use picking machines. But when to pick?

Judging just the right moment can be tricky, and many vintners use a refractometer, which looks like a small telescope, to determine the amount of sugar in the grape. Additionally, the time of day that is best for picking is also critical with many vineyards, particularly in warmer climates, opting for night picking as the sugars are more stabilized.

Now for the fun part—crushing, though not many

places still rely on human feet to do the work. After having most the stems and leaves removed, the grapes are crushed in large bins to separate out the skins and seeds. Now here is where the process differs a little for white or red wines. For white wines, the juice is extracted from the grapes, but the skins are left behind. With red wine, the skins and seeds are lightly crushed and go with the juice to fermentation. If all grapes were just pressed without the skins, all wine would be white. It is the skins that impart the color. The aim of crushing is to split the skins and get those sugary juices, called the must, flowing.

Fermentation is where yeast eats the sugar and produces alcohol and carbon dioxide. There is natural yeast on the grapes, and if left alone they would eventually ferment on their own, but often more is added to better control the process.

For red wines, as gases (carbon dioxide) start to be released, the skins will float to the top. Winemakers tamp these back down to keep them submerged as for full-bodied, bigger reds good exposure of skins in the juice is vital.

Now, for red wine, once fermentation is complete, the grapes are pressed. For a sweeter wine, the winemaker may stop the fermentation process before all sugars are converted, but for a dry wine, all the sugars is converted to alcohol and thus sweeter grapes produce higher levels of alcohol. Also, at this point the winemaker can add more sweetness or acidity to the wine if they choose. For a rosé, the skins are left in the juice for only a short time.

With the next step, aging, there are also many variations possible, with every tweak producing a different wine. Wines can be aged for a few months to several years; they can be aged in stainless steel vats or in oak barrels, and the oak can be new or used or American or French or even charred. Lots of variations.

The winemaker determines when this stage of aging is complete and it is ready to be bottled. For most whites that is only a few months, for most reds it is eighteen months to two years, at least. The wine is then clarified and filtered before being bottled.

Clearly throughout this process, timing is key: when to pick the grapes, how long to leave the must, watching the fermentation, and determining how long to age. All these affect the outcome.

But another major part of a wine's characteristics happens even before the grapes are picked, and that is the terroir.

Terroir is something most have us had heard of but maybe we are not exactly sure what it means. The actually word is difficult to translate properly, which is why we call it terroir and not an English equivalent.

At its most simple, it means 'sense of place.' But really terroir is a concept that revolves around climate, terrain, and tradition. Each terroir is unique as each has a unique combination of a number of factors: the grape, the soil, the mineral deposits, the sunlight, the rainfall, the altitude, the farming practices, and traditional techniques.

Each wine growing area has its own terroir and though many areas will grow the same grape, the wines will taste totally different.

Each wine bears the mark of its unique beginning, or terroir, which is why drinking an Oregon Pinot Noir will be a very different experience from drinking one from Burgundy.

Many European winegrowing countries have further organized this concept of terroir by legally delineating certain areas and the wine that is produced there.

Though there are several layers of appellations in the top three wine producing counties, the most common include France's "appellation d'origine contrôlee" (AOC), Italy's "Denominazionedi Origine Controllata" (DOC), and Spain's "Denominacion de Origin" or (DO).

This is why a true Chianti can only come from Chianti, a Rioja from Rioja, and true Champagne can come only from Champagne; a sparkling wine made from the same process will be called something else depending on where it is from.

4 GEOGRAPHY OF WINE

This notion of geographical regions can lead to confusion for those who have decided to take up wine drinking. Sometimes labels are based on the grape and sometimes they are based on the place. Shoppers can see on the same shelf one label from California that says Merlot and one next to it, from France, says Bordeaux. If you do a little homework, you will learn that these are both Merlot wines, so why the difference?

It is because Old World wines, that is wines from Europe, are generally labeled as to their location, or terroir. In the New World (basically everywhere else in the world) labels are usually by grape varietal.

For example, a Pinot Noir grown in Oregon is labeled Pinot Noir. It might mention the vineyard location, say Willamette Valley, but the primary labeling displays the grape. But if you want a French Pinot Noir, you'll need to know to look for a red Burgundy, as most red Burgundies are made from Pinot Noir.

By putting the place or appellation, sometimes

down to the smallest vineyard, on the label, the winemaker is acknowledging that because the wine was grown and made there it will have unique characteristics.

Thus, a little background checking is required if you want to know more about that bottle from Europe. Now, there is nothing wrong with being adventurous and plunging in because a bottle label is just appealing or the price is right—there is something to be said for being adventurous—but if you want to know the primary grapes involved, here is a quick rundown of some the most popular appellations in the top three wine producing countries:

France:
- Burgundy (Red) - Pinot Noir
- Burgundy (White) – Chardonnay
- Chablis – Chardonnay
- Beaujolais – Gamay
- Bordeaux – Blends of either primarily Cabernet Sauvignon or Merlot
- Cotes du Rhone – Blends, primarily GSM (Grenache, Syrah, and Mourvèdre)

Italy:
- Chianti – Primarily Sangiovese, can be up to 20 percent Cabernet, Merlot, or other varietal
- Super Tuscan – Not a DOC (appellation); these are generally Sangiovese with Cabernet & Merlot, or an Italian version of a Bordeaux
- Soave – Primarily Gargenega

Spain:
- Rioja (Red) – Tempranillo or blend of Tempranillo and Garnacha
- Priorat – Primarily Garnacha (Grenache in most other places)
- Cava – Sparkling blend of Macabeu, Parellada and Xarel·lo

Those three countries—France, Italy, and Spain—produce over 54 percent of the world's wine. Way behind those three, contributing only a 5 percent share of wine produced, is the world's fourth largest producer—the United States. And within the states, California is responsible for 90 percent of the yield.

Over a hundred varieties of grapes are grown in four main grape growing regions there, but the two primary grapes are Cabernet Sauvignon and Chardonnay. Just behind the United States, coming in fifth, is Argentina with its Malbec and Chardonnay. Australia is sixth; their predominant red grape is Shiraz, known elsewhere in the world as Syrah. And unsurprisingly, Chardonnay is the top white grape there as well. Germany is next with primary production centering on Riesling, and South Africa is eighth with their specialty—Chenin Blanc. A list of the top ten grapes produced worldwide has a few surprises.

No surprise however, concerning the world's most popular grape—Cabernet Sauvignon. It grows well in most climates, except vineyards far north. It is full-bodied, evoking the flavors of black cherry and baking spices; it is also loaded with tannins, those organic compounds in the wine that create an astringent mouthfeel.

When something is high in tannins it is referred to as dry. Sometimes, as a way to make Cabernet a little less astringent, it is blended with the second most popular grape in the world—Merlot. Merlot is widely grown in France, California, and Chile.

It too is full-bodied but has fewer tannins and the fruit comes through a bit more. The third most popular grape, Airen, is probably one you have never heard of. It needs a hot dry climate and is mostly grown in Spain where it is used to make brandy. Tempranillo, another Spanish grape, comes in at number four and is gaining in popularity in California, South America, Australia, and New Zealand. It sports aromas of dried fig and, sometimes, leather. It has a lighter acidic taste but is still considered full bodied. When a wine is described as full-bodied it generally means it has a complex mouthfeel—it will stay around in your mouth for a bit after swallowing.

Chardonnay is fifth, perhaps unsurprisingly as it is grown in nearly every grape-growing country. It is popular because though it is drier than many other white wines, it has full body with medium acid. Many people pick out notes of pear, or apple, or even toasted caramel or butterscotch. Syrah comes in sixth. It is grown in Australia, where it is called Shiraz, as well as France and California. Syrah has a more moderate amount of tannins, hints of black pepper or plum, and, incidentally, is the highest of all wines in anti-oxidants.

It is closely followed by another medium-bodied red—Grenache. In Spain it is called Garnacha Tinta, and it is low in acid with a hint of spiced berries. It is a medium-bodied red that is frequently used in blends.

With Sauvignon Blanc, the eighth most popular grape in the world, we are back to whites. Sauvignon Blanc is widely planted in France's Loire valley, Italy, California, New Zealand, and South Africa. It has a higher acid level and is very citrus-ey, with grapefruit being frequently predominant.

The next most popular grape is also white and, like Airen, may be one you have never heard of—Trebbiano Toscano. Though originally from Italy, it is now also widely grown in France where it is called Ugni and is used for brandy and calvados. It makes a refreshing fruitier white and is often blended with other grapes.

The last of the top ten, but not least to many, is Pinot Noir. Very big in California, France, New Zealand, Chile, and Australia, Pinot Noir often is fruit-forward with a color lighter than other reds. It is more moderate in tannins, so it is not too dry and is often used in blends.

5 BUYING WINE, STORING WINE & READING WINE LABELS

The first step in drinking wine is obvious—buying it. But where is the best place?

If you are lucky enough to have a local wine shop, please frequent it! The employees will, hopefully, love to give you their thoughts and are usually more interested in getting you a good wine at a good price (so you will return) than in selling you an overpriced bottle.

When you enter the store, have a general starting point for what kind of wine you want and a general price range in mind. There are a lot of really good everyday wines out there for under $13 a bottle.

If you want to pick up a bottle at the grocery store, some experts list Trader Joe's and Whole Foods as good bets as they usually have a fairly knowledgeable staff and, at least in Trader Joe's case, good values.

If you don't have either of those about, or are just at your regular grocery store, it may take a bit of looking about as sometimes they are arranged by varietal and sometimes by geography. A good plan is to bypass the big name Chardonnays and Cabernets and look for some interesting smaller or overseas vineyards. Keep an eye on the vintage.

Most grocery store stock is not meant to be cellared for years so look for the newest vintages. There may be some older hidden gems, but unless you really know what to look for, keeping with newer wines is a reliable tip.

Many wine-loving people buy at Costco, and they are the largest seller of wine in the United States (followed by Trader Joe's). Selection may be limited at times, and the staff may not be particularly helpful in this area, but once you begin to know a little more about wine you can sniff out the deals for yourself.

For those who are new to wine drinking, the safe bets may be the blends. Whether red or white, most blends will not be too far to the side of dry or sweet. If you want to try a varietal, two great grapes to start with are Pinot Noir for a red and Pinot Grigio (or Gris) for a white, as they have medium body, are not too tannic, and are good food wines. So faced with all these wine choices, where to start?

You start by reading the labels. Now this may not be as easy as it sounds. Old World bottles, as they denote appellation, can seem very unfamiliar.

By using the label below as an example, let's read through it and find out what it all means:

OLD WORLD LABEL:

Grand Vin du Bordeaux – This means the chateau says this is their best wine, *2005*– The vintage

Chateau La Point Chanteraille – The vineyard

Saint-Emilion – The appellation, telling you where it comes from, or the terroir. This label still says 'contrôllee' (AOC); under new EU ruling labels they will soon read 'Protégée' (AOP) but it means the same thing. This gives you the biggest clue as to what kind of wine it is.

In this case, as we know that Saint Emilion grows primarily Merlot, so even though this may be blended (maybe 5 percent) with Cabernet Franc, it is basically a Merlot.

Elevé en Fûts de Chêne - Literally, 'aged in oak barrels'

P. Estager – The name of the proprietor or owner of the vineyard

13% vol. – The alcohol content.

Mis en Bouteille au Chateau - This means all production happened on the estate. Grapes grown, wine made, and bottled. In Spain this will have the word Embotellat and in Italy Imbottigliato, but it will means the same thing.

Product of France – Just in case you aren't sure where the noted appellation is located.

NEW WORLD LABEL:

Chateau Montelena – The winery

he Montelena Estate – The vineyard; sometimes just the winery is listed.

Cabernet Sauvignon – The grape varietal. Under American law, if one grape is listed, the bottle has to contain at least 75 percent of that grape. That means it could have up to 25 percent of something else (usually Merlot), but that does not have to be listed.

Napa Valley – Instead of AOC or AOP, the States have AVAs or American Viticultural Areas. It is like an appellation in that it connotes that the wine comes from a particular (usually good) area. If an AVA is on a label, 85 percent of the grapes in the bottle have to come from that area. Under California law, if the bottle says California, 100 percent of the grapes must be from the state.

1999 - Under law, if a year is listed, 95 percent of grapes in the bottle must be grown that year.

Grown, Produced, and Estate Bottled – As in the French bottle, it means everything happened on the estate— grown, made, and bottled. The grapes were not brought in from somewhere else and their grapes were not shipped out to be made into wine elsewhere.

13.9% - Alcohol by volume. As the average is about 11.6 percent, this one is a bit 'heftier.'

Bringing Your Bottle Home

After buying the bottles and bringing them home, where is the best place to keep them? While you certainly do not need a cellar for everyday wine drinking, there are a few basic pointers to keep in mind:

Heat and light are the enemy. Try to keep the wine under 70 degrees, preferably about 55-60 degrees if possible, and away from vibrations and movement. But if you are drinking it in a short time this is not as much an issue as it is for longer storage. Just try to keep your wine from any swings in temperature.

Also keep them from light, especially sunlight and fluorescents, so if you can keep your bottles in a cupboard or closet, all the better. And you should try to store them on their side as this helps keeps corks from drying out.

White wines can just be chilled before serving, no need to store in the fridge (unless, like some of us, you like to have an 'emergency' bottle at the ready).

Once you have opened a bottle, recork (or wrap the top in plastic wrap), and pop it into the fridge, even if it is a red. Use them up within three to five days and let red wines come up to room temp a bit before drinking.

6 WHAT TO PAIR WITH YOUR WINE

Let's drink! But what to eat with that precious bottle you just bought? Some foods seem to be almost designed to go with certain wines. But there is a school of thought that argues if you like the wine and you like the food, they will probably naturally go together, so just enjoy!

But if you looking for a few tried and true ideas, try these classic pairings:

Cabernet

In one word: beef. Cabs are usually big and intense and with their tannins and acid levels can be a good balance for rich foods. As richer dishes, like lamb and beef, coat your mouth, a swoosh of Cab clears it away and readies it for the next bite.

Slow-cooked short ribs, brisket, a thick steak, or even meatballs—they all pair well with the tannins and structure of a nice Cab. Other meats also pair well, especially gamier dishes like duck and lamb.

But Cabs can be paired with more than meat—a rich mushroom stroganoff or a gooey mushroom pizza both pair with it really well. If you want a good cheese pairing, try a creamy blue, maybe a gorgonzola, or a big cheddar.

Merlot

Because it is a bit more 'middle-of-the-road,' it is a safe bet with so many foods. It pairs well with grilled meats, like pork chops, burgers, and even grilled swordfish or tuna. If you are having a rich sauce like a béarnaise or a Pasta Bolognese, Merlot is a good choice, and it would be great with a Shepherd's pie or a crispy roast chicken. Cheese-wise, pair it was a nutty emmentaler or other 'swiss,' a muenster, or a nice smoked cheddar.

Pinot Noir

Some foods you may think of as good matches for white wine, like brie and salmon, also pair really well with Pinot Noir. Because it is lighter than some other reds, it lends itself well to a greater degree of flexibility. Try a Pinot with any chicken or duck dish or some of those dishes you are never sure what to pair with, like a baked ham or even a lentil curry. A nice cheese match is a creamy cambozola.

Spanish red

If you picked up a Rioja (Tempranillo), think sun-drenched Spanish dishes and you won't go wrong. Chorizo sausage, vegetable ratatouilles or tarts, potato dishes, all work well, but try it with other warm weather foods and you'll be pleasantly surprised, like dishes with tomatoes, corn, or even your favorite Mexican food. For cheese pairings, these reds go great with all cheeses but why not try a couple of Spanish favorites like a Manchego (sheep's milk) or a Garrotxa (aged goat)? The same holds true for Italian reds. Why tamper with success? Next time you have spaghetti, crack open a Chianti!

Other reds

Grenache is going to pair quite well with everything that a Pinot Noir does. And for a Syrah (Shiraz), try it with some of the suggested Merlot or Cabernet pairings. Just remember that wines that are higher in alcohol need bigger foods. Lightly steamed dishes or plain poached items will be bowled over by most red wines. For most lighter dishes, whites are still the best choice.

Chardonnay

For the best pairings, it depends on if you have a big oaky bottle or a lighter leaner Chard as there are many differences depending on the part of the world and winery preferences. Most Chardonnays go really well with buttery dishes or those with a cream sauce; they are also great with shellfish, chicken, or pork. This is not the wine to have with Asian or spicy foods.

For good cheese matchups, with the oakier Chards you can go with a blue or a sharper cheese, for the cleaner chards, Camembert or a nice fontina or gruyere are good choices.

Italian whites

These are perfect with cheesy pastas, vegetable dishes, fish stews, and veal. Again, think of the area it was born in and those foods will naturally pair well. For a perfect cheese pairing, splurge a bit on a pecorino tartufo (laced with truffles)—perfecto!

Sauvignon Blanc

Because these often have herby notes, they go really well with any dish where herbs play a big role. They are also a good choice with some of the milder fish like tilapia or trout (or even a crispy fish sandwich) and can be perfect for a veggie quiche, or a shrimp salad. Best cheeses will include soft goat cheese, fresh mozzarella, or brie.

Rieslings

Though German wines have not been covered here, they make a great matchup for that difficult food group—spicy dishes and Asian or Thai foods.

For those dishes you do not want anything too oaky or tannic and want to go with crisp and maybe a little fruity. Riesling fits the bill as does Gewürztraminer and Viognier. Another great pairing for spicier foods are, surprisingly, bubblies, like Moscato, Prosecco, Cava, or even Champagne. It's not just for mimosas anymore.

7 CONCLUSION

As you start on your next wine adventure, remember to make note of those wines you like.

Take a picture of the label or write down the info. You may think you will remember what you like, and conversely what you didn't, but you won't.

This will serve as a valuable starting point for choosing your next bottle, and your next, and your next...

ABOUT POCKET GUIDE CLUB

Gain new skills fast with our insight-packed pocket guides. Our award-winning team of writers, researchers and historians simplify complex topics, doing the fact-checking and research for you, saving you time and money.

Each one of our Strategy Guides for Life® focuses on just one topic, explaining it in a fun, easy to read and engaging way, helping you learn fast without the overwhelm. Discover fascinating facts and gain tons of practical skills you can start applying today.

Plus, with every guide you buy, we donate another guide to someone else.

Shop all of our guides at:
www.pocketguide.club